Bubbles for Peace

With best wishes.

Dennis   2013

Dennis Evans lives and works in East Finchley, North London. His family roots are in Pembrokeshire, Wales. His poetry has been published in the UK and in India in English and Urdu translation.

In 2004, he travelled with his companion to the North East of Brazil. There they arranged and participated in a public reading with eighteen other poets from the State of Pernambuco, to raise money for the street children of Recife.

Dennis teaches poetry at the East Finchley Writing Workshops which he set up in 1990.

His dance poems have been choreographed and performed at Sadlers Wells Lilian Baylis Theatre, London.

He enjoys reading poetry in public and has read at a variety of venues which include: Edinburgh Fringe, arts festivals, public houses, literature festivals, multi-lingual gatherings, churches, The Millennium Dome, public libraries and theatres.

His previous publications include:
'Earth Anchor' Celebration Press (collection)
'Paper in the Wind' (pamphlet)
'The Cross-Country Run' (pamphlet)
He is a member of The Poetry Society, The Urdu Academy, English PEN, The Institute of English Studies, University of London and The East Finchley Open.
He gardens, walks and plays pool with friends for relaxation.

'I have read his poems with pleasure,

and I hope that his serious and

principled work will find readers here

and abroad. Poetry like his should have

international appeal.

No other epoch needed its poets more

than this one.'

John Rety
Torriano Meeting House, London

'...bubbles, such bubbles.
Bubbles for peace.'

My thanks:

To Lourdinha for all her encouragement, and
preparing the manuscript.
To Heidi for typing some of the poems.
To Jonathan for formatting.
To Heather and Pamela for proof-reading.
                                    &
To the Milly Apthorp Charitable Trust for help
towards the publishing costs of this collection.

Acknowledgements:

Some of the poems in this collection have
appeared in the following publications:
De Numine (University of Wales)
Faith and Freedom (University of Oxford)
The Inquirer
Second Sight (anthology)
Fragments
The Archer
Celebration Press

Bubbles for Peace
Dennis Evans

Celebration Press

Published 2005 by
Celebration Press
58 Helen Close,
London N2 OUU   UK
Tel:(020) 8346 9528

ISBN 0 9531298 1 0

Cover (front & back)
'Camden Institute batik studio'
            by
        Dennis Evans

Printed by Cpi
38, Ballards Lane
London N3 2BJ

British Library Cataloguing in Publication data.
A catalogue record for this book is available
from the British Library.

Contents:

1   You
2   A time for release
3   Dogs
4   Rupa
5   Old friend
6   Landscape
7   A time of roses
8   Phenomena
9   Beloved
10   The first casualty
11   Celebration
12   Beacon
13   Rhodes
14   The dance
15   Me and my groups
16   Letter to a friend (for John)
17   Keeping the peace
18   Letter to a friend (for Roy)
19   The gift
20   Sandcrab
21 - 22 The diamond
23   The journalist
24   Moving on
25   Concern from government
26   A poem for St. David's Day
27 - 28 Counting
28   Calpe
29   The anointing
30   Clerihew
31   Wrong time
32   Dewi

contents contd.

33   Silence
34   New music
35   Beach, song, peach.
35   Not cricket!
36   All the people
37   Friend
38   Bequest
39   Caution
40   Circling
41   Woofing
42   Bouquet
43   Flying in a different way
44 - 45 Knowing my place
46   Home front
47   The meeting
48   Basílica
49   Untitled
49   Rose
49   Graffito
50   Visitor
51   The transformation
52   At the gallery
52   An ordinary man
53   Gardens
54   Botanists' friend
55   A is for Autumn
56   Haiku for Margaret
57   Cheese!
58   Surrender
59   Haiku for Mary
60   Boxed-in
61   Letter to my student

contents contd.

62   Mountain walk
63   Kantouni
64   Food for thought
65   Happy Christmas!
66   Song for myself
67   Second sight
68   Questions
69   Stone Circle
70   Bubbles for Peace.

You

I'd forgotten how beautiful you are,
had seen you on my last year's walks:
naked, arms aloft
silhouetted against blue-gold skies.

Fingers curled like a dancer's,
rooted in your being.

Clad in Autumn remnants
you blaze like a cathedral
in this early-morning winter light.

A time for release

A time for release,
peace between them.
Long years of waiting,
two saplings and a tree.

Tree shaded saplings from the sun,
showered them with his leaves in autumn,
protected them from chill east winds.
In turn, they warmed him with their gracefulness,
blew against him,
caressed him with their branches.

Left together they will die,
branch and root entwined.
Time for uprooting,
shooting into the unknown.

Dogs

Opportunistic politicians scramble for Peace Wagons.
Go to ground after votes,
go to ground after votes.

Unelected leaders sanction killing of children.
'War is fun,
war is glorious.'

Night-vision glasses for impaired politicians.
'We can see! We can see!'

We can see orchestrated killing by a colonising nation,
mouthing slogans, mouthing slogans.

Cities burn,
whilst politicians earn obscene fees and salaries.

Our school children articulate
the great nation's conscience.

Orchestrated murder by civilised nations.
Dogs of war, men of straw.

Rupa

Balanced in wood
and bought in Woolworth,
or was it Bankok?

Here for so long,
placed on the shelf by a friend,
'For fun', she said.

Matchbox-buddha,
viewed through half-closed eyes,
made life-size,
I feel the weight of your presence.

Object of focus,
of calm, of majesty;
leading to silence.

Old friend

You have seen much,
and such that you would never tell.

Have smelt good meals,
been present in good company.

Are the centre of attention,
keeping us apart by the right amount.

Lost during the break-up of our marriage,
I claimed you back
with a fierce sense of ownership.

When you collapsed,
our daughter played doctor
mending your leg whilst I assisted.

Old friend, with your heart of oak,
you have seen much
and such that you will never tell.

Landscape

Molten sunlight on the water,
where red-sailed schooners track the river.

The sea-wall bears us through the mudflats,
past empty hulks now long-forgotten.

Silence lies across the landscape,
the flowers incline toward Aeolus*.

Aeolus: Ruler of winds (Homer)

A time of roses

I am in the harebell,
and the hawthorn.

I am in the devil's-bit
and yellow coltsfoot.

I am in the blue,
the blue of the footpath geranium.

I am in the landscape;
a time of roses.

Hucklow

Phenomena

' And darkness covered the face of the earth '

The garden is like a low-lit stage,
in cold green light
We all have complimentary tickets.

The sun struggles to retain his supremacy,
his moon gently insinuates.

The birds have stopped singing,
and flowers are closing
as though for the night.

The sky moves lower.

Passing cars swish,
like rollers up a darkened beach.

Beloved

I dream you through the Winter;
in your beginning I need you.

In all your newness you are here;
I dream you through the Winter.

Stay with me Beloved,
be my other lover.
Anoint me with your fragrance,
reveal your glow.

I dream you through the Winter,
in your beginning I need you.

The first casualty

Where is truth now,
propaganda rules OK?

'A quick war, that's how!'

Where is truth now,
if we 'liberate' people and towns
of a nation we attack today?

Where is the truth now,
propaganda rules OK?

Celebration

I'm beginning to tip waiters and cabbies again,
family and friends are pleased for me.

I can pay the bills.
Each week, I used to worry.

Long may the work last!

Away from the walls of my open prison,
my students' demands sustain me.

I'm in touch with my pride and usefulness.

At the Job Club,
my erstwhile companions
still look for their 'leads'.

Now, I can hope for them.

Beacon

Symbol of my hoping and of my despair,
the mallow tree grows,
glows in the early-morning sun.

Cathedral of flowers:
home for birds and house cats,
refuge for fieldmouse and hedgehog.

It stands like a beacon,
guiding me back to base.

Rhodes

Thistle, fig, cactus
Second world war's defences
The land has conquered.

The dance

I watch the lilies straighten,
and the wheel turns.

Daffodils trumpet, heralding Spring!
And the wheel turns.

Grass is greener,
and the sun reaches through.

I am the hub.
And the wheel turns,
and turns, and turns...

Me and my groups

or
My groups and I

My feeling about groups is:
that every time I go to join one,
another appears on the horizon!

Not another one, I hear myself say.
Do I stay with that one or change?

My other feeling about groups is:
that you never know who is going to be there!

Gregarious ones?
Raucous ones?
Obviously cautious ones!
Undercover agents?

People in 'oil',
              'the city',
                 clover!

Socialists, democrats, publicans!

My feeling about groups is:
that every time I go to join one,
another appears on the horizon!
How about you?

Letter to a friend

(for John)

The Jazz fraternity is out in force
to support and take pleasure
In Humph's music tonight.

Witty as ever, he jokes with the Band.
Now, left foot forward,
he leans back and blows...
Just as I knew he would.

Saxophones, in conversation,
are playing Bach-like.
'Like making love', Mari says.

'Do nothing 'til you hear from me..,'
the trombone replies.
Until you hear from me, Mari.

Just as I hoped it would,
the Band plays 'Bad Penny Blues.'

I remember your stories
of a band I'd never heard.
Of you, with your love of conversation
and company, treating your audience
to histories of old standards,
being hurt when they heckled.

How's the big Band in the sky John?
Don't ask me why, I'm close to tears.

Keeping the peace

Peaceful protesters

Mounted police redundant

Good humour saves confrontation.

London Peace March
22nd March 2003

Letter to a friend

(for Roy)

The cotoneaster is established
and the broom is in flower
but the sweet-scented roses
have gone to their maker.

Your poetry and etchings,
both large and small,
still hang in the hall.
Admired by Johny,
enjoyed by me
and appreciated by all.

I am looking forward
to extending the lawn.
Where cattle used to graze,
I now grow flowers.
Roses, fuschias,
climbers, bushes.
There are mallow trees and lilac,
lemon balm, violets.

I think of leaving,
decide to leave a mark.
Next year, a motorway will come
and I will be gone.

The gift*

I

An ancient place,
a field called Temple Croft,
haunted by wolves and wild boar.

Owned by a bishop,
and Knights Templars.
Taken by Henry.

II

Λ modern place,
in a borough called Barnet,
home to societies and university.

'Discovered' by my children,
its gardens a refuge.
Gifted by Henry.

Epilogue

Two Henrys.
One crowned, the other:
'the uncrowned King of Finchley'.

**Avenue House & grounds
Bequeathed to:
The people of Finchley by
Henry C. 'Inky' Stephens
1841-1918*

Sandcrab

Moving like a war chariot,
you scurry across dry sand.

Freeze at your burrow,
blend in with your landscape.

Then, like a conjuror's trick,
vanish at our coming.

Puri,   Orissa

The diamond
(for John, Sheila, John, Margaret)

We came together,
hands held, eyes closed.
Listening to the intoning, encouragement,
insinuation of our own white witch.

Paired off.
Looked at the other
each in his or her own way.

Separated...
Came together
looked at another
each in their own way.

Separated,
again and again
completing our circle.

Nothing said,
finally we parted
each to himself.
Each to his chosen place,
in contemplation.

And what did we see?
A mirror-image of our other self,
another's stance we would disown,
a vulnerability not outgrown?
The eager girl in her middle-aged face.
Qualities impossible to name.   *Cont. over*

cont.

The hand-touch giving support
facing you and you,
facing myself.
Time without end.

Agreed to silence,
we will never know.
Will we digest,
add to the diamond,
add to the glow?

The journalist

There was an old man from the press
who kept all the news up his vest.
When his boss got to know
he said:'You'll have to go,
you silly old man, you're a mess'!

Fleet Street

Moving on

Squat, green, spotted white,
seemingly at random.
Designed for symmetry.

Container, tool,
fun to hold.
Designed-asymmetry.

Bought for my children
on a weekend visit.

Left behind,
as they grew older.

Now, I feel that
it's almost mine.

I like its sound
when cutting lead,
laugh aloud
when it falls apart.

We have moved on.

Kalymmos

Concern from government

"We have published on the MoD website, the March 1999 paper on the subject"

Returning refugees, without protection,
trying to live in a land made treacherous
by depleted uranium shells: radioactive.

Returning refugees, without protection, trying to live
whilst soldiers in breathing apparatus and protective gloves
work on vehicles which were a threat to us.

Returning refugees, without protection, trying to live
in a land made treacherous.

A poem for St. David's day

Miracle of colour,
yellow above all other.

Daffodil, Daffodowndilly
trumpeting: Spring!

Counting

'Follow the steam and you'll find it;
strip to your underwear, put on the boiler suit!'

Saturday, winter.
Ten babies at risk on the ward.

So, head first into the duct:
concrete below, above, at either side.

Inching forward, steam fills the space.
His torch: useless.
He pictures the location.

At the corner of the duct his body sticks.
Concrete above, below, at either side.

Panic, like steam, scalds him.
Fear supplants breathing.
He wants to burst free, scream...
Concrete above, below, on either side.

He knows that he'll implode,
crushed by his own strength.

He remembers his mentor.
It holds him in tension.
He counts:'One, two, three...'   *Cont. over*

cont.

Sweat mixed with fear surrounds him,
'eight, nine, ten.'

His skin becomes snake-like;
he ripples around the corner.

Calpe

Yellow as the Sun,
the cactus is in flower.

I wait in the shade,
Old Bougainvillea looks across.

The rock commands the high ground.

Valencia

The Anointing

I lay down the tool of my reason,
watch seasons turn,
and the eagle swoop.

I watch confusion in my mind,
await its silence;
await its clarity.

At the sand-union of earth and sea,
incoming waves anoint my feet.

Puri, Orissa

Clerihew

Said Van Gogh:
'The reason my ear is off
is because it's a good vessel for paint,
next to the trestle.'

Wrong time

We met at the wrong time.
You,
with your shine and girlishness,
me,
with my forgotten need.

I thought you'd be my other lover.
Apart,
I feel my need.

Singing in the void,
you come apart at the seams,
cascade into a pit of forgotten despair.
Scorched by the flames,
I hold you,
listen to your story.

Dewi

He talks of church music,
literature, art;
mutual friends,
and paranoia.

Bearded, pipe-smoking,
he smells to high heaven!

A derelict, not caring,
good women tried to save him.

Silence

'Behold the lilies of the field...'

Sitting with cornflowers
in a field above Hucklow.

Butterflies for companions,
the village is before me.

A farmer's-wife patchwork
laid out on the fields.

Hill forts and burial grounds,
I rest in the silence.

New music

Here's another week,
much busying to be done.
Craft seven new spokes.

And nothing is changed:
you present the honeypot,
we gesture, strut, preen.

Taking refuges:
in Buddha, Dhamma, Sangha.
Good start to the day.

Taking refuges:
in Buddha, Dhamma, Sangha.
Good end to the day.

One day at a time,
the edge of understanding.
I plunge and I plunge.

And in our sharing
we have become as children,
gone back to our roots.

I am the hub,
busyness revolves about me.
The day is mine.

Beach, song, peach

Two fat ladies far down on the beach
decided to screech and to screech !
When asked what was wrong,
they burst into song
and proceeded to swallow a peach:
each !

Not cricket!

The player with only one ball
said, 'I wish that it wasn't so small.'
When he came out to bowl,
he fell down a hole
that worried young man from Porthcawl.

All the people

All the people I have known
and been known by,
all the people I have shown
and been shown by:
are now no more,
on another shore.

We are poor without each other
like a sister without a brother
or a mother without a son.

All gone, yet all one in the brotherhood
and sisterhood of man.

Friend

A silly thing to say, I know,
but my garden has become my friend.

As long as I'm here the friendship will grow,
a silly thing to say, I know.

The weeding, pruning and the flowers I grow
give me more than the time I expend.

A silly thing to say, I know,
but my garden has become my friend.

Bequest

A tribute to Henry Moore

Always your request.

Reclining before trees

Looking to the bridge.*

* *'Sham bridge' at Kenwood.*

Caution

Twelve Summer poets,

together sharing the muse,

many 'clerihewd'.

Circling

There are nine of us,
circling before rain.
Not saying much,
just the nine of us.

Dip, dive and glide,
yes He knows we are at play again.
There are nine of us
circling before rain.

Woofing

Painting is done by painters.
Logging is done by loggers.

Rocking is done by rockers, and chairs.
And pogging is performed by large potato eaters.

Benedictine is made by monks,
getting 'plastered' is achieved by drunks.

However 'dogging',
with consent but
resisted by farmers,
is performed by couples.

Woofing, is done by dogs.

Bouquet

The winter jasmine is early,
curling along the wall.
A present from you,
in your previous life.

A life of parties, intense talk,
and open marriages.

She, came to me like a waiting bride.
You, played the other part.
Left us alone,
slept with her husband.

She comforted me,
journeyed through my nightmare-nights.
Later, you slept with her.

A bouquet of confusion,
and yellow winter flowers.

Flying in a different way
for John

Her protector from childhood,
Angel-man appears again.

Man of iron, Angel-man,
risen from a desecrated landscape.

Protector of the landscape and its people,
children play safely at his feet.

Atlas-like,
his back supports our worlds.

Poised for flight,
he'll be flying in a different way.

Hucklow

Knowing my place
(A poem for two voices)

He: And knowing my place
       I behaved like a man.
       Painted the house, gardened.
       Protected her, our children,
       the old people.
       Meals were always on time,
       shirts nicely ironed.
       Crying was weakness,
       meekness unmanly.
       I worked in a factory.
       Thought, this is my life.

She: Knowing my place
       I behaved like a woman.
       Looked after the house, shopped.
       Cared for him, our children,
       the old people.
       Housekeeping money was always on time,
       went on holidays.
       Crying was womanly,
       meekness a virtue.
       I looked after our children.
       Thought, this is my life.

Both: When we were thirty

She: I became liberated

Contd. over

44

cont.

He: She became liberated.
        Not knowing my place,

She: But knowing my place.

He: I behaved like a man.

She: I behaved like a sister.

He: Protected her, our children,
        the old people.

She: Raised my consciousness.

He: Painted the house, gardened.

She: Went on marches,
        supported the movement.

He: Meals were never on time,
        shirts rarely ironed.

She: Wages for housework!

He: Crying is manly,
        meekness a virtue.

She: Male domination!

He: Intellectually, I understand...

Home front

Soldier-chrysanthemums glow,
illuminating late afternoons.
Defending Autumn,
last line of defence against Winter,

Independent, gregarious.
Tolerant of a single rose.
Soldier-chrysanthemums glow,
illuminating our late afternoons.

The meeting

The column approaches;
a column of fire.

Unsuspecting waves sculpt rocks,
remembering earlier forms.

The wind drags on a plastic sea.

A sense of stirring,
the Psychic shudders.

The column approaches,
a column of fire.

Basílica

(Bom Jesus de Matosinhos)

'In a sea of hills', you said.
Above iron-red earth.

Elevated, set against palms.
A place of chapels, and of sculptures.

A place of miracles, and none.
I wept to see the cripple
on the Basílica steps.

A place to live,
and a place to die.

Stations of the Cross,
and the love of Christ.

The spirit of Aleijadinho* surrounds us.
The Way of the Cross and prophets,
brought to life by his hand.

The heat of Jerusalem,
and Golgotha hangs over us.

**Antônio Francisco Lisboa da Costa, sculptor,
architect and builder. Known as 'Aleijadinho'
(little cripple).*

Congonhas do Campo, Minas Gerais, Brazil.

Untitled

Beautiful in black.

Where have you flown in from?

Heralding the Spring.

Rose

Eager, yellow,

held in water.

Celebrating Summer.

Graffito

'Amanda is a Les',
the spray-paint said.

But what about Les, I thought,
is he a Manda?

Visitor

Immediate, proud,

anemone at the door.

Eastern visitor.

The transformation

For one second,
the World held its breath.

For one second, all was silence...
For one second,
God held His breath.

In that second,
in that silence
the World was transformed.

At the gallery

Read all about!
Read all about!

With catalogues at the ready,
they wander hand-in-hand through the gallery.
Reading every word in case they are heard
voicing an opinion of their own.

An ordinary man

He is not the nicest of men,
nor the worst.

He is just a troubled man,
who thought himself accursed.

Gardens

Gardens are for playing in,
lying in.

Gardens are for working in,
shirking in.

Gardens are for planting in,
chanting in.

Gardens are for praying in...

But best of all,
gardens are for playing in.

Botanists' friend

Dinosaur snacking

Munching for posterity

Earth's oldest tree.*

Ginkgo biloba

A is for Autumn
(for Class 4H, Edgware Junior School)

A is for Autumn,

U is underneath the trees.

The wind blows, conkers fall.

U is underneath the trees.

M, a full-rounded harvest moon.

New season follows high summer.

Haiku for Margaret

Autumn memories,

hidden in the recipe,

your good apple cake.

Cheese!

Devon:
beaches,
war-free.

Kids crawling under barbed wire
with no fear of enemy fire.

Pulled back, scolded:
'...danger from land mines!'

Shingle, smooth enough to run on.
Sandcastles and beach cricket.

Friends and family relaxed, cheerful:
'Oh, I do like to be beside the seaside...'

Sitting with our toes turned up,
looking at the camera.

Surrender

Held together, like ancient barefoot dancers,
we breathe the same air.

Breast to chest, each is the mother
the other did not have.

Covered in your kisses,
I balance on your feet.
Give myself up to the God in you.

Haiku for Mary

Golden oranges

Memories of Algarve groves

Mary's marmalade.

Boxed-in

The Gallery has locked him in,
put him in a box.

Did he sin?

The Gallery has locked him in.
He's suffering for 'Art', not sin.

Small boys bang on his home, create shocks.

The Gallery has locked him in,
put him in a box.

Letter to my student

Dear Miss Wallenborn,

Welcome home to Britain.

The Muse awaits you.

Mountain walk

Cheese and grapes,
grapes and bread.

Bread and you,
you and grapes.

Grapes and cheese,
cheese and bread.

Smell of pine,
smell of you.

Mountain track,
coastal view.

Water's wetness,
bread and you.

Kantouni

At Ursula's Restaurant Bar,
foreigners who have travelled very far,
sing:
'Happy birthday to you...'
just at the start of 'Zorba the Greek...'
What a cheek!

Food   for   thought

Put
not your
faith in our
politicians.
They are genetically modified!

Happy Christmas!

Buy food!
Buy drink!

Buy presents!
Buy, buy, buy..!

Bye-bye bank balance.

Song for myself

I was sure I knew it all,
but there was you.
Showed me how to work by hand,
gentleness with me and other children.

I used to think I knew it all
when I met you.
You taught me priorities,
how to choose.

I used to think I knew it all
when I met you.
In my despair you taught me
how to dance by myself
and with others.

I assumed I knew it all
till I met you.
In the park you showed me poplars
moving like dancers in the wind.

Oh yes, I thought I knew it all.
But there was you,
and you,
and you...

Second sight

I've seen it all now,

I've been to a vision therapist!

Questions

Will you walk with me,
talk with me?

Will you plant with me,
chant with me?

Will you work with me,
shirk with me?

Will you play with me,
lie with me?

Will you climb with me,
rhyme with me?

Will you...;
will you be my Valentine?

Stone Circle
for Karen

Built on the hill,
cattle have reclaimed the land.

At the centre lie the stones,
positioned above dissimilar rock,
driving energy round the circle.

*'Join us, sacred site,
join us to the past.'*

A bridge to the centre,
its entrance and exit astrologically defined.

*'Join us, sacred site,
point us to the future.'*

The murmuring ditch, now dry, held water;
cleansed worshippers at this site.
A barrow contains their ancestors.

*'Join us, sacred site,
join us to the present.'*

Bubbles for Peace

There were Reverends and Rockers,
housewives and children.

There were old friends and new friends,
politicians, policemen.

There were Christians and Muslims,
Communists and Buddhists.

And banners, such banners,
banners for peace.

There were dancers and drummers,
and children in pushchairs.

There were priests and our poets,
and grannies in wheelchairs.

There were students and stiltwalkers,
and a brave paraplegic.

And a man with his toy gun,
lit by his laughter,
blowing bubbles, such bubbles.
Bubbles for Peace.

London Peace March, 15th February 2003.